Dwayne Brain

Hi, there, kids. This is your friend, Uncle Bob. Say, how much do you know about your Central Nervous System? That's the part of you that thinks. It's your personal computer. Let's see who just arrived.

Hello, kids. I am your brain, the world's greatest computer.

Dwayne Brain, welcome.

Thanks a lot, Uncle Bob.

Dwayne, tell the guys and girls about your job.

Uncle Bob, my wise Creator put me in charge of all your body parts. I make sure that they work together smoothly at my command.

Wow, what an awesome computer! Thanks for all you do for us, Dwayne Brain. The kids and I are curious. How much do you weigh?

In a ten-year-old, I weigh about two pounds. You kids will have an adult-sized brain when you're fifteen. I'll weigh three pounds then.

Explain to the boys and girls what you look like, Dwayne.

I look like half of a walnut when it lies on its flat side. I'm even wrinkled like the nut.

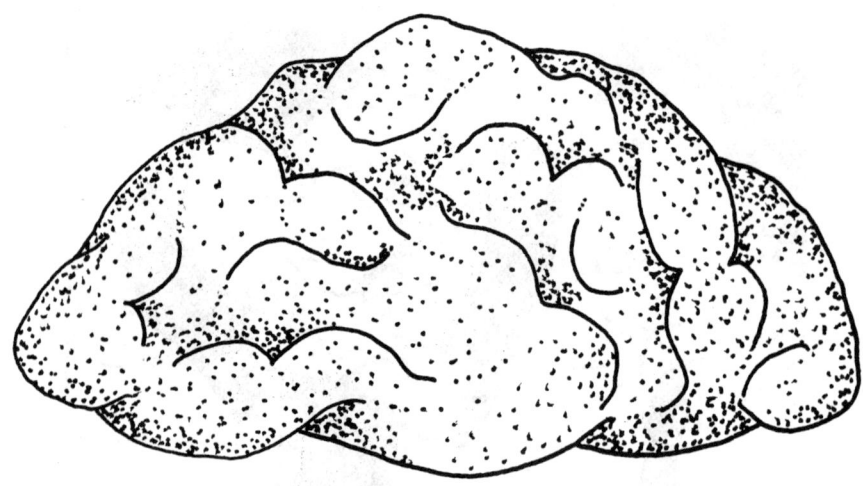

Uncle Bob Talks With My Central Nervous System

By Bob Devine
Barbara Cunningham, Illustrator

Before you turn on the tape,
meet Uncle Bob and three members
of your Central Nervous System:

Dwayne Brain, Seymour Spinal Cord, and Nellie Nerve.

Uncle Bob talks to one of them
in each section of the tape and book.
Listen and follow along as
Uncle Bob visits with:

Dwayne (page 3), Seymour (page 18),
and Nellie (page 34).

Here's how Uncle Bob's words look.
Here's how Dwayne, Seymour, and Nellie's words look.

Now turn on the tape and
meet Uncle Bob.

Chariot Books
DAVID C. COOK PUBLISHING CO.

Chariot Books is an imprint of David C. Cook Publishing Co.
David C. Cook Publishing Co., Elgin, Illinois 60120
David C. Cook Publishing Co., Weston, Ontario

UNCLE BOB TALKS WITH MY CENTRAL NERVOUS SYSTEM
© 1985 by Bob Devine for text and Barbara Cunningham for illustrations.
All rights reserved. Except for brief excerpts for review purposes, no part of this book may be reproduced or used in any form without written permission from the publisher.

First Printing, 1985
Printed in the United States of America
90 89 87 86 85   5 4 3 2 1

Library of Congress Cataloging in Publication Data

Devine, Bob.
   Uncle Bob talks with my central nervous system.
   Summary: Dwayne Brain, Seymour Spinal Cord, and Nellie Nerve explain the body's central nervous sytem.
   1. Central nervous system—Juvenile literature.
[1. Nervous system] I. Cunningham, Barbara, ill.
II. Title.
QP370.D48   1985   612'.82   85-5721
ISBN 0-89191-945-7

Acknowledgements
Thanks to Robert White, M.D., Neurosurgeon, Cleveland Metropolitan General Hospital, for the hours he willingly gave me just talking about the brain.
To Matthew Likavec, M.D., Neurosurgeon, Cleveland Metropolitan General Hospital, who likewise spent hours explaining how the spinal cord and nerves function. A special thanks to Dr. Likavec for going over the three chapters in this book and verifying their accuracy.
Thanks to Jon Weingart, M.D., Neurologist, Akron City Hospital, for the time he spent explaining the function of nerves and the spinal cord to me and also for going over the manuscripts of the three chapters and giving me his approval to their accuracy.

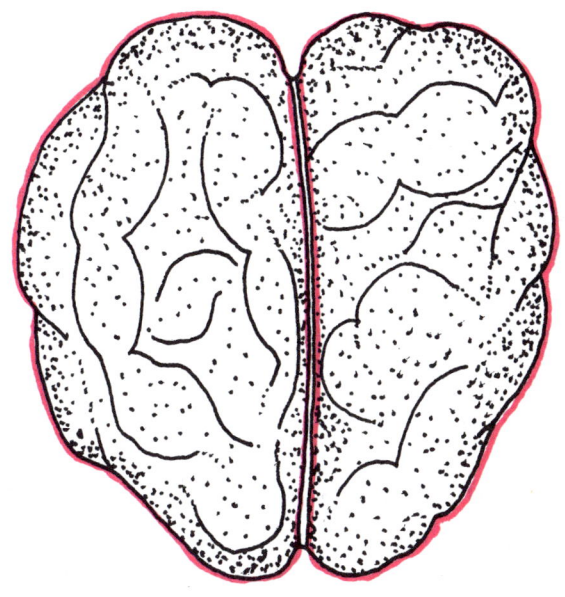

Why are you so wrinkled?

My wise Creator God knew he could pack more brain cells in a small area by wrinkling me. If all my wrinkles were smoothed out flat, your brain would be two and a half feet square.

So by wrinkling you, the Creator God was able to pack an awesome amount of material in a small place. Dwayne Brain, as I look at you from the front, it looks as if you're divided right down the center.

That's exactly the way it is, Uncle Bob. You're looking at my cerebrum, my right and left brains. Now, kids, to help you understand me better, imagine two sections of an orange that are still attached.

Hey! You do look like two sections of an orange. I never thought of you as being two brains, Dwayne. I always thought of you as just one.

You have *two* brains working for you, kids. But the Lord wired them together so they *share* information, like two computers would.

I've heard that my left brain makes the right side of my body work, and my right brain makes my left side work. Is that true?

It sure is. Hold up your right hand, kids. Your left brain made your right hand go up. Now, swing your left foot back and forth. OK! Your right brain made that left foot move. Move both feet and wave both of your arms. This time, both sides of your brain were working for you. Say, "Hello, Dwayne Brain."

Hello, Dwayne Brain!

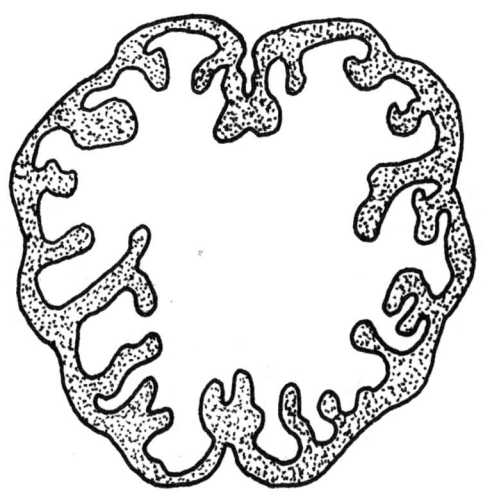

Your left brain made you talk!

Dwayne, sometimes people say their brains are full of gray matter. What do they mean?

The gray matter is my wrinkled outside layer. It's only one-eighth of an inch thick. It's the part of me that controls all your thoughts and actions.

Are your brain cells located in this area?

Oh, yes. My gray, wrinkled matter is crammed full of neurons. Neurons are microscopic brain cells that can record special information. Neurons are the most important part of me!

How many neurons do the girls and boys have, Dwayne?

One hundred billion.

Wow, that's 100 with nine zeros after it! Dwayne Brain, you said your neurons can record special information. Tell us what you mean.

They've been programmed to act like librarians, Uncle Bob. Kids, you know how a librarian makes out a card for each book in the library, files the card, and places the book on a shelf?

Sure, they understand that very well.

My neurons do that for everything you see, hear, touch, taste, and smell. Everything you do is very carefully sifted and identified by my neurons. Then it is given a special computer code and put on my shelf.

That is mind boggling, Dwayne Brain. Where do your neurons store all of this information?

Point to your left ear. Now point to your left eye. OK, this special library shelf is right there, between your left eye and ear. It's full of neurons that store all of your memory.

How difficult is it for your library neurons to find one tiny piece of information out of the billions of pieces stored on your shelves?

They can find it easily, Uncle Bob, usually within one second. You see, the Lord designed my neurons to work together. They ask one another questions and share information with each other.

How do they do this, Dwayne?

Neurons do not touch one another. Powerful microscopes have shown that when one neuron wants to talk with another neuron, it has to send its message over a tiny gap.

Keep going, Dwayne, this is like an exciting adventure!

To send its message, the neuron makes a special chemical that contains its question. The chemical jumps across the gap to the other neuron. That neuron shoots a chemical answer back over another gap. This happens millions of times every second in your brain, Uncle Bob.

What an incredible computer, Dwayne Brain! Would you give the kids and me an example of how this works?

Sure, if someone were to blindfold you and hand you an apple and a baseball, could you tell which one was which?

Of course we could.

But, there was a time when you couldn't. There was a time when you first learned what apples and baseballs were. Perhaps when you were very young, your mother said, "Here's an apple. It's good to eat."

Yes. I took the apple, felt its shape, and smelled it. Then I tasted how good it was.

When you did that, your hand sent the feel of the apple to my neurons, your nose gave them its smell, your mouth sent up the taste, and your ears brought the word apple.

So all four pieces of information went to your neuron library. What happened then?

The neurons carefully studied it and checked to see if there was anything like this on their shelves. After a few seconds, they discovered this "apple" was brand new to them, so they put all these facts about the apple on my special memory shelf.

OK, Dwayne. Now what happened a week later when Mother said, "Close your eyes, and hold out your hand. Now, feel it! Smell it! Can you guess what this is?"

You said, "It's an apple!"

What happened inside your gray matter to tell me that I was holding an apple?

My neurons picked up the feeling of the apple's firm shape in your hand. Other neurons nearby received its smell. All the neurons studied that feeling and smell, flashed chemical questions back and forth over their gaps, and compared the feeling and smell with the ones stored on their shelves. The neurons agreed, "We had this same feeling and smell last week. It is an apple." It took my neurons less than a second to tell you what you were holding.

Do your neurons work the same way for everything I learn?

Yes, they do. When the teacher asked you a question, you said, "Ooh, I can't think of the answer." So the teacher gave you a clue. That was all you needed. When your ears sent that little clue to my neurons, they recognized it from what you studied last month and gave you the answer. A second later you said, "I know!"

But before those neurons could dig out the correct answer, they had to have it on their library shelves.

That's right, Uncle Bob. Your neurons study every bit of information the teacher gives you, kids. The better you listen, the better your neurons will remember.

What a neat computer, Dwayne. So what the kids and I put into your neuron library is mighty important.

Yes, the things you read or see on TV or in the movies all go into my library.

Along with what I hear on records, tapes, and the radio, plus all the conversations I have.

If you pour garbage into me, you're going to get garbage out of me, kids. It's as simple as that.

But if the gang puts good quality information into you, Dwayne, then they'll get good information out.

That's it, Uncle Bob. I guarantee you, boys and girls, if you put good things in me, like the Bible, you'll get good things out.

Dwayne, do all 100 billion of your neurons work in the library?

No, not all of them. I also have motor neurons. Now, kids, a motor makes something move. That's what my motor neurons do. They make electricity and cause all the muscles connected to your skeleton to move.

Oh, like the muscles in my legs and arms. Dwayne, if these motor neurons are in your gray matter, how do they send their electricity down to my body muscles?

My white matter carries the electricity to your spinal cord.

Your white matter?

Yes, right underneath my gray matter there's a lot of white matter that is made up of billions of nerve fibers.

What are nerve fibers?

They're like special insulated wires, Uncle Bob. The ends of these wires connect to my motor neurons and carry the electricity to your spinal cord.

Wow, so without the billions of nerve fiber wires in your white matter, your motor neurons could not help the rest of my body.

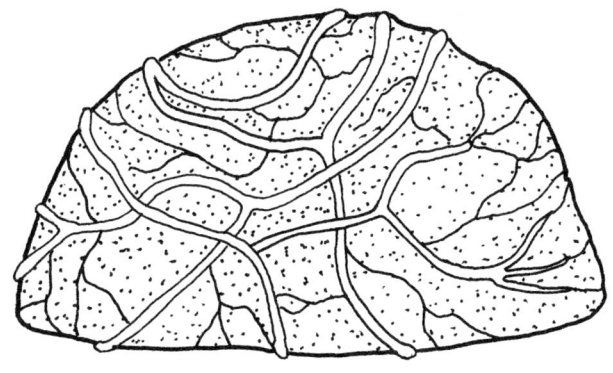

Neither could my sensory neurons. These neurons pick up the five senses: sight, sound, taste, smell, and touch. If the Lord hadn't put these neurons in me, I'd never know what's going on outside of me.

And I wouldn't be able to see, hear, taste, smell, or touch. Dwayne, where do your neurons get the energy to do so much work?

Christ my Creator put miles of blood vessels on top of my gray matter. They feed my neurons oxygen and sugar. That keeps them working.

Dwayne, such a super computer as you must be well protected. How did Christ the Creator protect you from getting injured when I bump my head?

He floated me in a salty liquid called spinal fluid.

Is that like a shock absorber, Dwayne?

Not like one, it is one! If you didn't have it, I'd be injured the first time you took a step. You'd jar me, and I'd quit working.

How is this fluid held in place around you, Dwayne Brain?

By a strong rubbery sheet, or membrane, that the Master Designer wrapped around me. It's called the dura.

Then, around the dura the Creator made my skull?

Yes, your skull is very thin, but because of its shape, it is very, very strong, Uncle Bob.

Dwayne Brain, thanks for being my guest today.

Thanks for having me, Uncle Bob. Kids, remember. Be careful what you let in me, because it's there for life. Fill me with good things about Christ my Creator and you'll do great. I promise!

Seymour Spinal Cord

It's time for another neat visit from one of the members of our Central Nervous System. I wonder who's here today.

Greetings, boys and girls. I'm your spinal cord. If you didn't have me, you would be numb from your neck all the way down to your toes.

Seymour, is that you?

Yes, it is, Uncle Bob.

Seymour the Spinal Cord, welcome! Tell us what you look like.

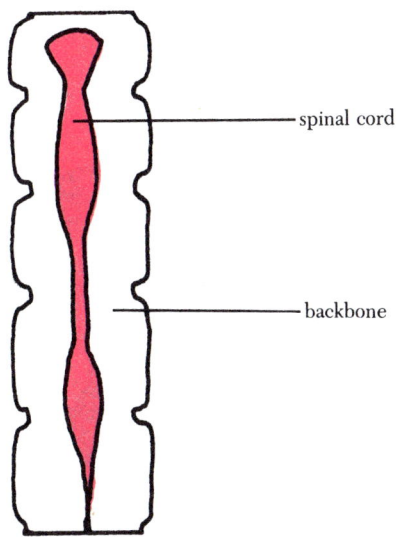

I'm a white cord about a half an inch thick and 18 inches long. That's how big I am in a ten-year-old, and I'll never get any bigger.

Seymour, you're thicker at one spot—about one-fourth of the way down.

Yes, the Creator designed me that way. He packed a lot more special cells in me right there. They make your legs and arms move.

What are you made of, Seymour? And how do you stay alive and healthy?

I'm a fibery material that is packed full of nerve cells and nerve fibers. Most of my food comes from your bloodstream, Uncle Bob. Blood vessels pass through nearly every joint of your backbone and attach directly to me.

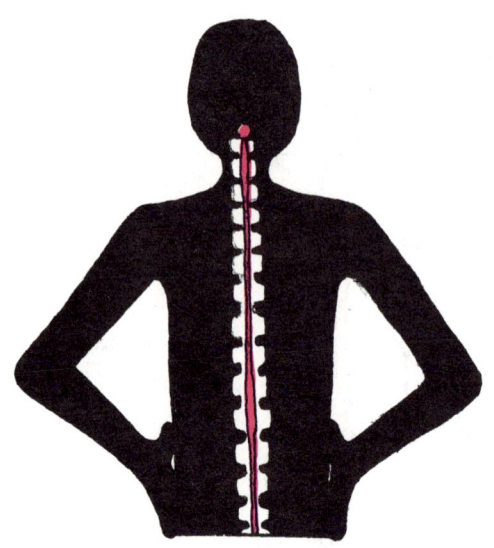

Where are you located, Seymour the Spinal Cord?

I'm tucked inside your backbone, and I bend with it every time you bend.

That's neat! What do you do for the kids and me?

I'm like a cable that has billions of wires in it. The top of my cable connects to your brain. The wise Creator designed me to carry the signals from your brain to all of your muscles.

So really you're an electrical cable between my brain and my muscles.

Yes, billions of short electrical signals leave your brain every second and travel through me.

Wow! How fast does this electricity travel through you?

Three hundred forty miles an hour.

Wow! That's really moving. Where does the electricity go?

It goes to 31 pairs of spinal nerves the Creator attached to me. Nerve fibers from all over your body are attached to these spinal nerves. The nerve fibers carry the electricity to all of your skeletal muscles.

Skeletal means skeleton, right?

Yes, Uncle Bob. The electricity causes the muscles to move these bones, like your legs, feet, arms, and hands.

You make me really appreciate you, Seymour.

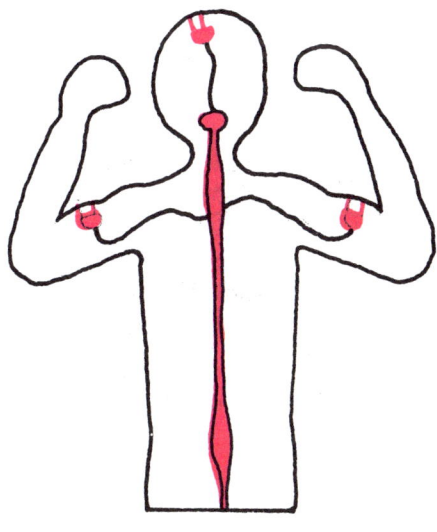

Just thank my Maker, Uncle Bob. Kids, wiggle your toes and fingers at the same time. Do you know what happened? Your brain heard me and sent electricity down my cable to your fingers and toes.

So it's because of you that the girls and boys can run and jump.

But that's only half of what I do for you, kids. I also receive important signals from your skin and carry them up to your brain.

Would you explain that, Seymour?

Sure, the sense of touch travels up me to your brain. So do the feelings of hot and cold.

So that information travels through you to let my brain know what's going on outside of it.

Right, Uncle Bob. One bit of information you kids send through me a lot is how tightly you hold something.

Tell us about that, Seymour Spinal Cord.

Kids, imagine you're holding on to the handlebars of your bike. Now that feeling of holding the handlebars travels through me and into your brain. The brain has learned from past experiences how tightly you should squeeze the handlebars. It sends that message back through me to your hands so that you hold on tightly enough to control the bike.

I'll remember that the next time I ride a bike, Seymour, and so will the girls and boys.

Just remember, kids, that's me helping you!

Right on, Seymour. The kids and I thank you.

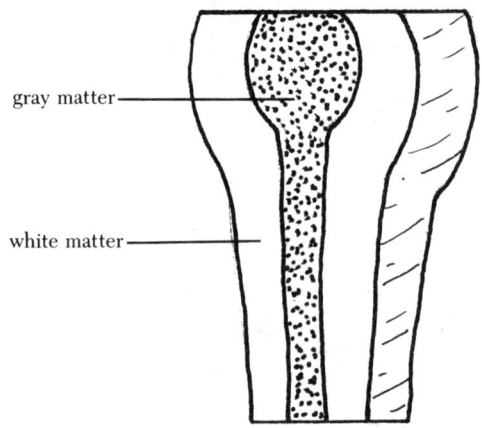

I'm just doing what my intelligent Engineer designed me to do.

Seymour, is your cord white all the way through?

Oh, no! My center is gray. It's filled with billions of important nerve cells and neurons that make your muscles work.

So you're white on the outside and gray on the inside.

That's right. I'm made of white and gray matter, kids.

Hey, so is my brain. But my brain is gray on the outside and white on the inside.

Just the opposite of me. And did you know my white matter is attached to the white matter in your brain?

No, I didn't, Seymour.

My white matter is made of billions of wires that carry all the signals to and from your brain. Sometimes 100 million signals pass up and down me at the same time.

Hey, that's neat, two-way traffic! Seymour, your white matter is super busy! What is your gray matter like? Is it connected directly to the gray matter in my brain?

No, it isn't, Uncle Bob. My white matter carries all of the information from your brain and gives it to my gray matter. In my gray matter, billions of nerve cells give that information to my neurons.*

What do your neurons do with this information from my brain?

They give it to my 31 pairs of spinal nerves that carry it to the left and right sides of your body.

Does your gray matter do anything else, Seymour?

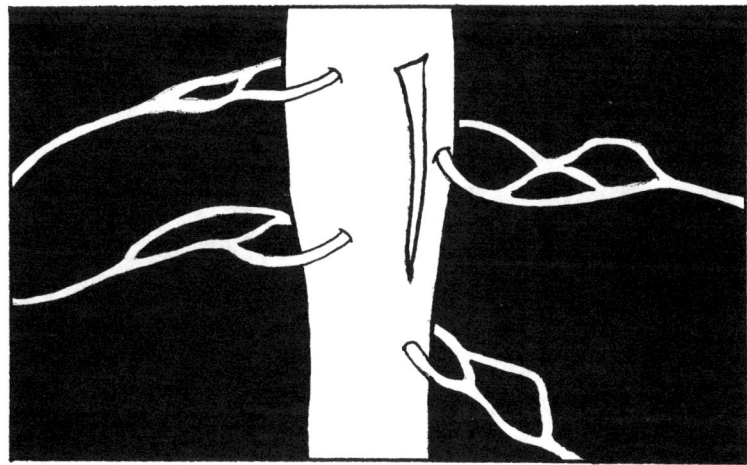

*Please turn the tape over.

Yes, indeed. My gray matter is called the nervous reflex center of your body.

What does that mean?

Reflex means to bounce back or return. If you kids put your finger on the hot stove, what would you do?

They'd pull it off very quickly! That hurts!

Boys and girls, I sent a message to the muscles in your arm and hand to pull your finger off the hot stove.

You told them? Not my brain?

That's right. Kids, when the nerve endings in your finger got burned, they flashed an emergency signal to the nerve center in my gray matter. Those nerve cells knew immediately where the trouble spot was, so they made their own electricity and sent it to your arm and hand muscles. They made you pull your finger off the hot stove.

So this is the reflex action of my spinal cord.

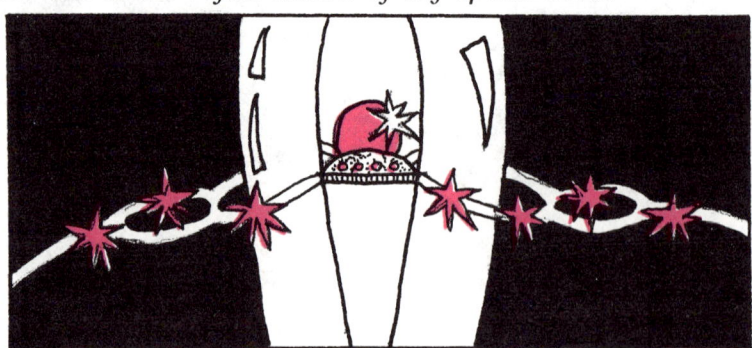

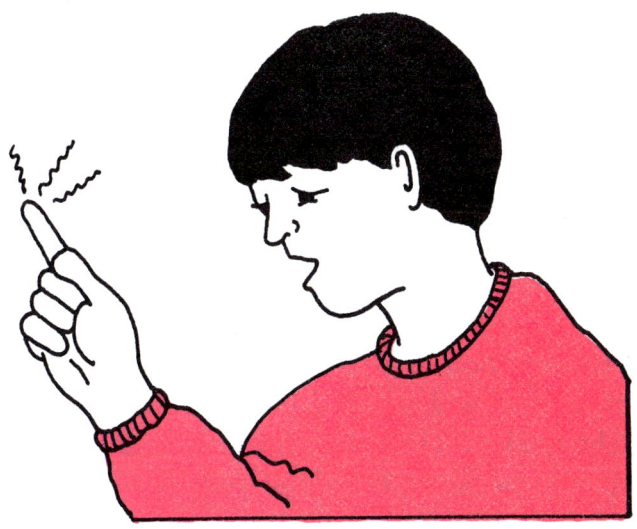

Yes, it's one of the most important jobs my gray matter does. It happens in less time than it takes to tell about it.

Why didn't my brain tell my finger to get off the hot stove?

That would take three times as long, Uncle Bob. The message would have to go all the way up me and into your brain. Then your brain would have to send an electrical signal down me and into the correct muscles.

I see now. You did it in only one-third the distance and one-third the time.

Kids, that's important, because if you kept your finger on that hot stove a split second longer, your burn would have been much worse.

Christ the Creator really cares about us, doesn't he, kids?

Seymour, you look a little like my brain. Do you have a left and right section, too?

Do you ask that because it looks like I'm divided right down the middle?

Yes, that's it.

When the Son of God made me, he made two, 18-inch spinal cords and attached them side by side into a left and right section. Then the Master Designer connected my left side to the right side of your brain.

And your right side to the left side of my brain, Seymour.

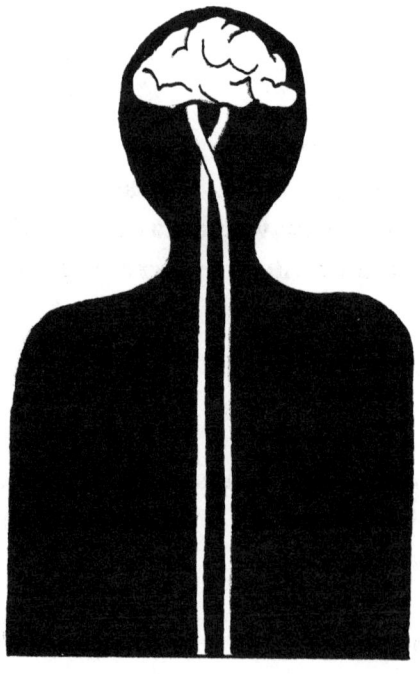

Yes, that's why the left side of your brain controls the right side of your body, and the right side of your brain controls the left side.

Seymour, how do the left and right sides of my body attach to you?

Remember my 31 pairs of spinal nerves?

Yes, does that mean one nerve comes out of your left section and the other comes out of your right section?

Yes, that makes one pair. I have 30 more pairs just like them all the way down my cord.

So, what happens to the electrical signals coming out of these left and right nerves?

Nerves from all over your body attach to them. The wise Creator connected them to the correct sides of me.

He's always correct, Seymour.

Each of my 31 nerve pairs is wired to me in two places. One connection carries information from your brain to your muscles. The other connection brings information from your body's senses up to your brain.

What a super design, Seymour Spinal Cord.

Each one of my 31 nerve pairs has 5,000 tiny wires inside. That makes it possible for so many different signals to go to and from your body muscles.

Seymour the Spinal Cord, it's really neat the way the Son of God has designed you. Surely, such an important part of my body must be well protected.

In a big way, Uncle Bob! The Creator made a strong backbone, or spine, and threaded me through it. If I were not inside that strong bone, the first time you bumped me, you'd squeeze me and hurt me. I'd probably quit working for you. And you know what that would mean.

I'd be paralyzed. Does only a backbone protect you?

Oh my, no! The Lord put three strong, cushiony layers of fiber lining just inside the backbone. I'm inside that soft, fiber lining, but the lining doesn't touch me.

What keeps it from touching you, Seymour?

Between the fiber lining and me, I have spinal fluid. It acts as a shock absorber to protect me from bumps.

So that spinal fluid is there to protect you.

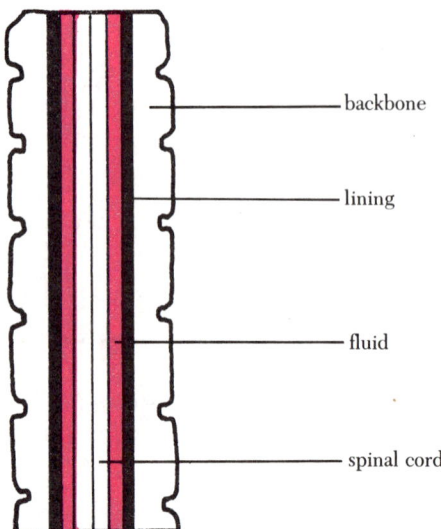

- backbone
- lining
- fluid
- spinal cord

Right, Uncle Bob. But it has two other important jobs, also. It keeps constant pressure on me. Without that pressure my nerves will not work. The spinal fluid also feeds me protein, potassium, sugar, and salt.

Neat, Seymour. Where does this spinal fluid come from?

It's made in your brain, Uncle Bob. There's a gland that produces spinal fluid. The same fluid surrounds and protects your brain.

How does it travel down into you, Seymour?

The place where I am attached to your brain has a tiny opening. The fluid flows down through that opening and circulates through me and back up to your brain.

So it's always fresh and full of good food.

That's right, the old fluid is removed and new fluid is added regularly.

I've learned so much about you today, Seymour the Spinal Cord. Thanks for teaching the boys and girls and me.

You're welcome, Uncle Bob. Kids, don't ever take me for granted.

We won't, Seymour. Kids, whenever you bend over, think about Seymour inside your backbone, and thank your wonderful Creator for the way he gets the signals from your brain to all your body muscles.

Nellie Nerve

Hi, kids, it's time to meet another member of our Central Nervous System. Let's see who just sat down at the microphone.

Hi there, Uncle Bob. I'm one of your nerves.

Nellie Nerve, welcome.

Thanks, Uncle Bob.

Nellie, are you nervous?

Yes, I've never talked into a microphone before.

Just relax, Nellie Nerve. We're going to have loads of fun talking to the boys and girls. The kids want to know what you do in their bodies.

I carry electrical signals from your spinal cord to your muscles. Without me, you couldn't move a muscle.

We couldn't even lift our little fingers without you?

Right, and you couldn't feel things, either. I carry senses—like the sense of touch—back to your spinal cord and brain.

So without you, my brain and spinal cord would not be able to send or receive these signals.

Exactly, Uncle Bob. I'm like an electric cable with thousands of tiny wires inside of me.

Thousands of wires, Nellie?

Oh, yes, Uncle Bob. Each wire is a lot thinner than one of your hairs, kids. My wires are in packs of 1,000 each.

Packs of wires! How many packs do you have, Nel?

Five.

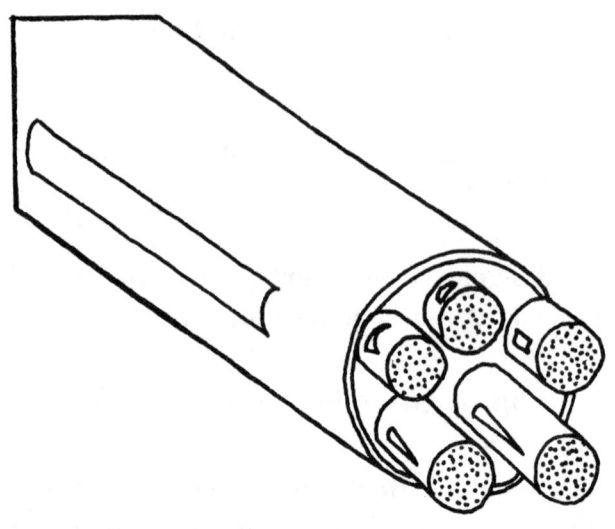

Kids, how many wires are inside Nellie Nerve?

They said 5,000, and they're right. Now that's just one nerve, kids.

Is each of these packs of wires like a cable itself?

Yes, that's a good way to describe me. I'm like a big cable with five smaller cables inside me.

Nel, where are you located? And how large are you?

I'm one of the three nerves in your wrist, Uncle Bob. In a ten-year-old, I'm a quarter of an inch wide. I look like a piece of round, white clothesline. I begin at your spinal cord, travel over your shoulder, down your arm and into your wrist.

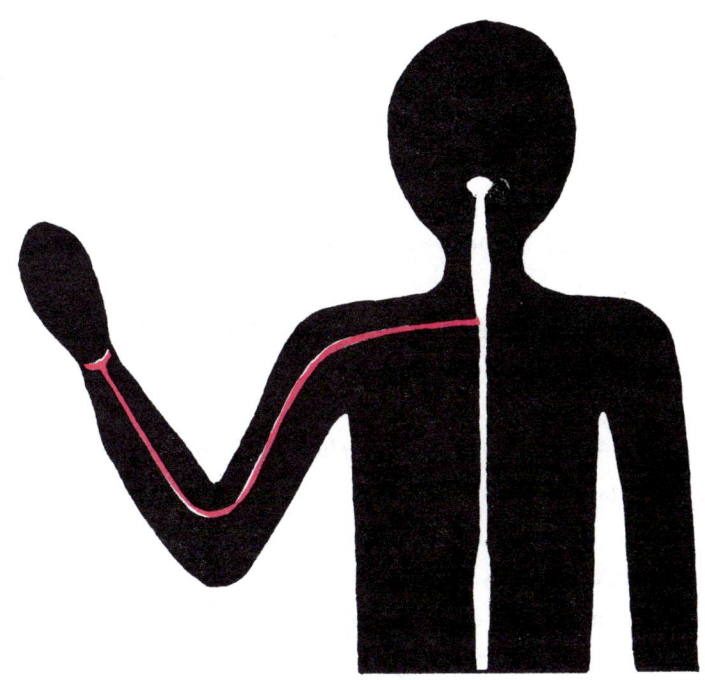

Wow, you're quite long, Nellie. That's awesome—how the great Creator packed 5,000 tiny wires in you.

Imagine trying to insulate each of those tiny wires, kids!

Yes, it'd be impossible, because each wire is smaller than a hair.

But each one is insulated, Uncle Bob! It had to be that way. The Creator God put insulation around every one of those 5,000 wires.

And that's just one nerve, Nellie. That's just you. What a great Creator we have, boys and girls!

There are many, many more nerves besides me, Uncle Bob. If you could see a picture of all your nerves, you would see hundreds of lines traveling all over your body from your nose to your big toe.

How many feet of nerves do the boys and girls have?

If you laid them all end to end, they'd be about the length of a football field, 300 feet.

Nellie Nerve, you said earlier that each one of your 5,000 wires is insulated. Why?

OK. A tiny jolt of electricity from your brain, lasting about a thousandth of a second travels down some of my wires. If there were no insulation on my wires, they'd touch one another. The electricity would get on all the wires. That would make all your muscles go bananas.

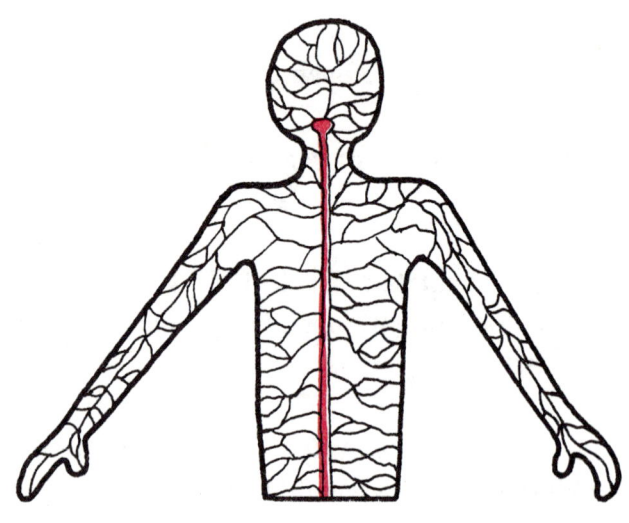

Really! Could you explain that, Nel?

Remember, I'm one of the nerves in your wrist. If all 5,000 of my wires were not insulated and touched one another, all the muscles in your hand would receive electricity. They would tighten. You wouldn't be able to pick up anything with your fingers. Your hand would be squeezed into a tight fist.

So, Nellie Nerve, if all those little hairlike wires short-circuited, I'd really be in a peck of trouble.

That's right. Thank God for your myelin.

My who?

Your myelin. That's the name of my insulation. In fact, it's myelin that gives me my white color.

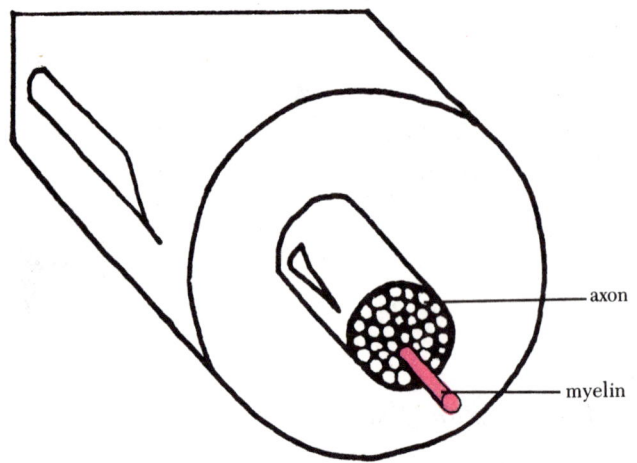

Neat! Nellie, let's investigate those 5,000 tiny wires inside the myelin. Do they have a special name?

Yes, each separate wire is called an axon.

An axon!

Yes. Kids, remember the myelin insulation around each axon wire? The Son of God, my Maker, wrapped a fiber around the myelin insulation. It's for my protection. A tiny axon is smaller than your hair. It needs to be protected, or your body is in trouble. The fiber protects it. But it does a lot more.

May I guess? Does it act like a second wire that completes a circuit?

Yes. Your muscles have to have two wires going to them, not just one. It's like an electric lamp.

That's right, there have to be two wires to that lamp or it won't light up.

And that's the way it is with me. My thin center wire is the axon. The outer fiber is my second wire, and the insulation is between the two. All three of these together are called a nerve fiber.

So one nerve fiber has insulation and two wires that carry electricity.

Yes, Uncle Bob and there are 5,000 nerve fibers inside of me.

Nellie, are you just beneath my skin, or are you deeper inside my body?

The very wise Lord knew I needed protection, so he put me underneath your muscles, right next to your bones. That's where I travel all the way from your spine, up your shoulder, down your arm, and into your wrist.

That is super protection, Nellie Nerve. My muscles protect you from bumps or shallow cuts. What else protects you?

You have a layer of fat and three layers of skin on top of me, too.

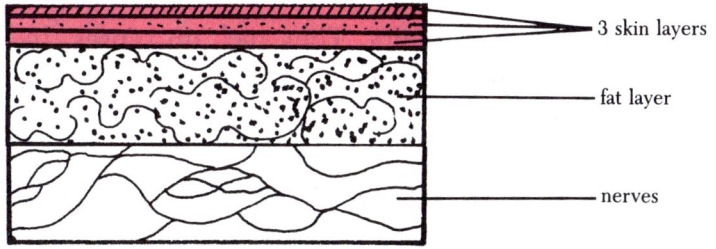

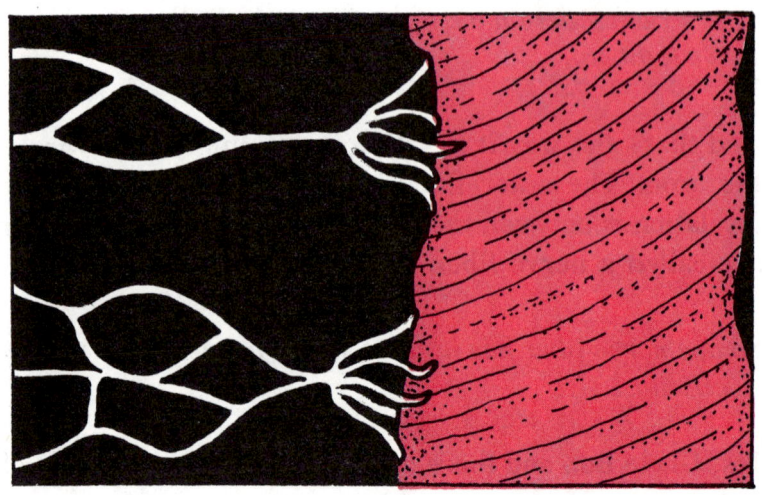

We do have a very intelligent Creator, don't we, kids! Nellie, a minute ago, you said your nerve fiber wires attach to my muscles.

That's right, my nerve endings look like little tree roots that attach to your muscles.

That's another reason for being located under my muscles, Nellie. You're closer to where you need to attach.

Right, Uncle Bob. Kids, remember those 5,000 nerve fibers in me? Only half of them make your muscles move.

What do the other 2,500 do, Nel?

They're called sensory fibers. They pick up senses, like hot and cold, and they send that information back to your spinal cord and brain.

So you have two-way traffic inside of you, Nellie Nerve.

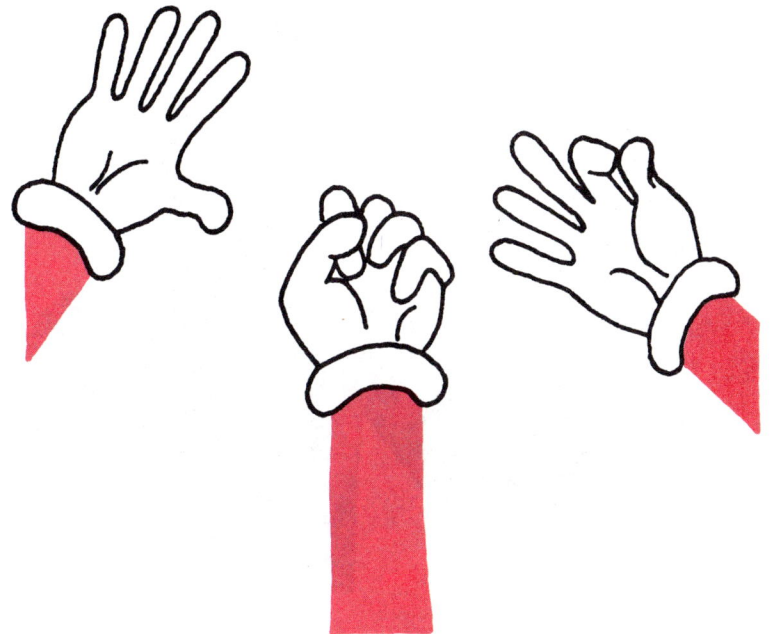

Indeed I do. Most of the nerves in your body have two-way traffic.

All of that inside a quarter-inch piece of "clothesline"! Nellie, why do we need so many nerve fibers?

Let's have the kids show us, Uncle Bob. Kids, hold your right hand out, palm up. Now wiggle your fingers really fast . . . good. Now make a tight fist. OK, open your hand, and touch each fingertip with your thumb. Next, close your fist and open it, close it and open it; keep doing that, and start wiggling your fingers while you do it. OK, you can stop.

I get it. We need all your nerve fibers to make all of those different muscle combinations in our hands work.

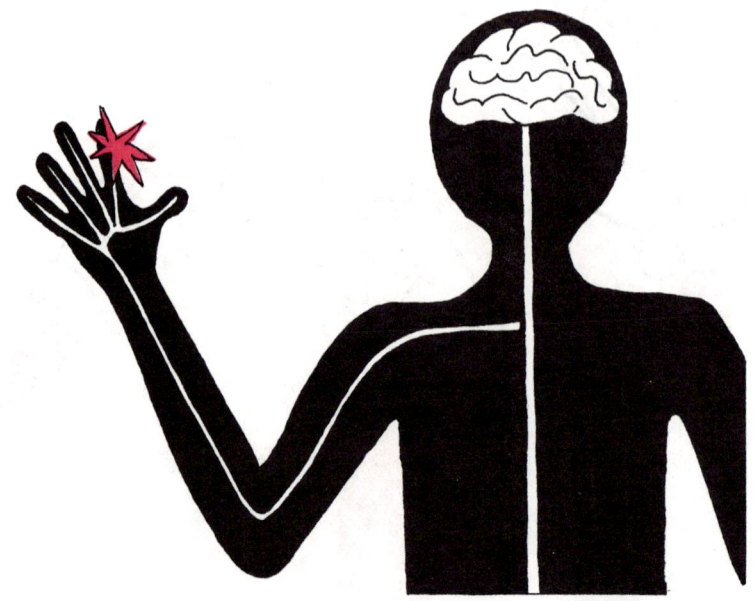

Yes, your brain sent the message to your hand to do all those things.

Nellie, how did that happen?

After you decided what to do with your hand, your brain sent the message to thousands of nerve cells in your spinal cord, kids.

And what did those nerve cells do, Nellie?

They all sent messages to *my* neuron in the spinal cord.

What do you mean, your neuron?

It's mine because it attaches just to me, Uncle Bob. All 5,000 of my tiny nerve fibers are attached to it. Each

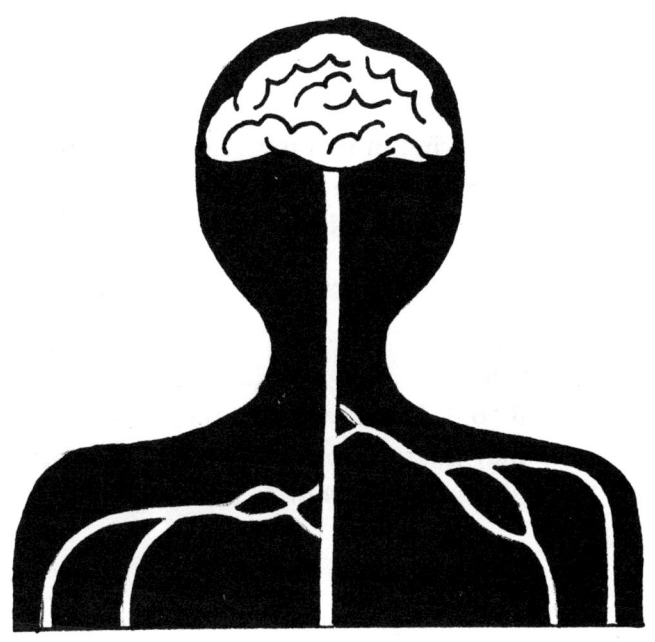

nerve in your body has its own neuron in the spinal cord.

Nellie, inside this neuron, do 5,000 nerve cells from my spinal cord attach to your 5,000 nerve fibers?

That's right. And your brain tells which spinal cord cells to carry electricity to my nerve fibers.

And, Nellie, because your 5,000 nerve fibers are attached to these cells, you can carry many signals from my brain or only a few.

Yes, whatever your brain decides. But to work like that, each little nerve fiber has to eat. It gets its food from a tiny blood vessel inside my cable.

Amazing! What do your nerve fibers need, Nellie?

That blood vessel gives me plenty of oxygen and sugar from the blood flowing in it. That's how I stay healthy, so I can carry signals back from the millions of receptor cells the Creator put in your skin.

What are receptor cells?

They're all over your skin to pick up your senses like touch, hot and cold. Whenever you touch something, the receptors in that part of your skin make electricity and send it through me up to your brain.

And presto, I have feelings, thanks to you, Nellie Nerve.

Right, Uncle Bob. Girls and boys, tickle the palm of your hand with your finger! Feel it? The receptor cells in your

palm made electricity, and I carried it to your spinal cord and brain so you could feel it.

Nellie, let's talk about the electricity you carry in the other direction for a second. Do the electrical signals from my brain make my muscles work?

No, the electricity doesn't actually make your muscles move, but it does have a very important part.

Would you explain that, Nel?

My neuron manufactures a very important chemical. It sends this chemical down through each of my 5,000 nerve fibers to tiny storage packets at my nerve ending.

Right where the nerve fiber attaches to the muscle, right?

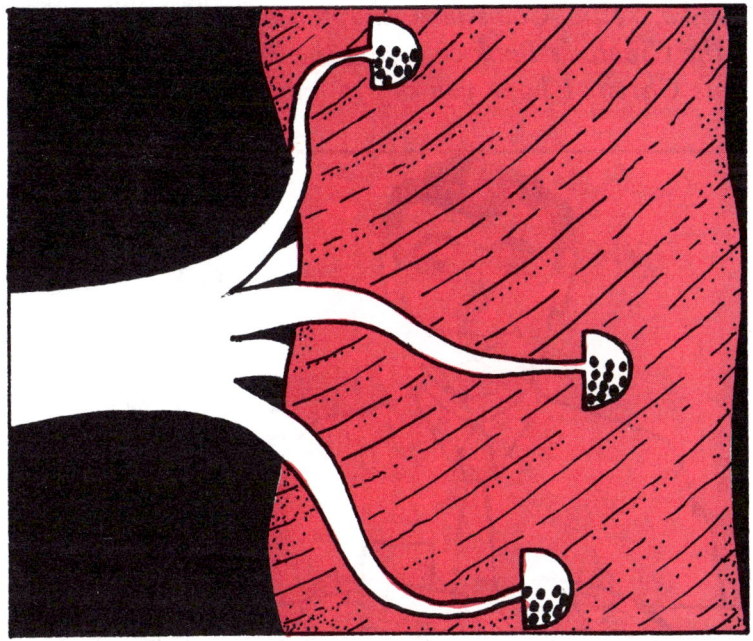

Yes. When your brain sends a quick electrical signal down my nerve fibers, these little packets release the chemical.

Where, right out your nerve endings?

Yes, right where they attach to the muscle cells. That little jolt of electricity makes me dump my chemical into the muscle you want to move.

That is so neat. So it's the chemical that makes my muscle move. Nellie Nerve, you have been one super teacher today. Thanks a lot.

It's been my privilege, Uncle Bob. Kids, I hope you can see your nervous system was made by someone very special, very wise and kind. I hope you know him.

Thanks, Nellie. Colossians, chapter one, verses 13 and 16, in the Creator's Book calls him the Son of God, the Lord Jesus Christ. I hope you get to know him and love him.